GW01388488

John

by
Jennifer Moorcroft

*All booklets are published thanks to the
generous support of the members of the
Catholic Truth Society*

CATHOLIC TRUTH SOCIETY
PUBLISHERS TO THE HOLY SEE

Contents

Renewal

The period in which John of the Cross lived (1542-1592) was a time of immense change and challenge for the Catholic Church. Protestantism was spreading all through Europe. In response the Church had convened the Council of Trent (1545-1563) to state its teaching clearly in response to the doctrines being spread by Luther and Calvin, and to renew the life of the Church, as well as the religious orders.

External changes alone could not renew the Church but internal renewal had already begun some years previously. It was an era when great saints arose. In Italy there were Philip Neri and Mary Magdalene de Pazzi; in France, Francis de Sales and Jeanne de Chantal; in England, Thomas More and John Fisher; in Spain, Ignatius of Loyola, John of the Cross and Teresa of Jesus, to name just a few. It was a reminder of the Church's single mission - to make saints of ordinary men and women and make them outstanding in their love for God.

In response, new orders were springing up, attracting men and women eager to advance in the spiritual life and to spread the faith. The most notable of these were the Jesuits, founded by Ignatius of Loyola. The existing religious orders were also beginning to reform, although as John and Teresa were to find out, not all their members were happy to have their comfortable lifestyle disrupted.

John and Teresa were Carmelites, an Order that originated on Mount Carmel, and which came to Europe when the Muslims eventually regained control of the Holy Land. Sadly, John and Teresa's efforts to reform their Order resulted in splitting the Carmelites into two branches: the Calced (or shod) Carmelites of the Ancient Observance, and the Discalced (or unshod), (founded by John of the Cross for-men, and Teresa of Avila for women), who - at least in the beginning - went barefoot.

Even more than the reform of their Order, John and Teresa, both Doctors of the Church, wrote spiritual classics on prayer and the spiritual life that have nourished men and women ever since, and are no less relevant in our own times.

Early Years

Soundbites have a habit of sticking, and a soundbite description John of the Cross has often been labelled with is that of 'Doctor of the Dark Night'. He has tended to be seen as world-hating, excessively austere and imposing impossible demands on those who seek to advance in the spiritual life. This is very far from the truth, and we can catch a first glimpse of his real character from his parents and the influence they had on him.

His father, Gonzalo de Yepes came from a wealthy and influential family in the Toledo region, although he himself was an orphan. He went to live with an uncle, who was part of the family's financial and mercantile interests, and eventually worked for his uncle, travelling all over Spain. Staying in Fontiveros during a business trip he met a young woman from Toledo, Catalina Alvarez. In a time when marriages were often of convenience, Gonzalo and Catarina fell in love, much to the horror of the Yepes family. Catalina was poor, of a lower class, but this was not the only reason for their opposition. Rumour had it that she was either the daughter of a Moorish slave, or else of someone who had been burnt at the stake for judaizing. If the marriage went ahead, it might have uncovered the fact that there was also Jewish blood in their own lineage, something they were keen to hide.

Despite this, the young couple were quietly determined in their love for each other, and were married about 1529. Gonzalo was cut off and disowned completely by his family, which meant that they had to make their own way in life and earn a living for themselves. Catalina was a weaver and taught her husband how to make lady's veils and bonnets and this provided them with a basic income. By the time John was born in 1542, their third son, his parents were providing him with an enduring example of a deep, sacrificial love at the heart of their family, of hard work and dignity in poverty.

Family tragedy

All the family worked together at their silk weaving. This made their house a factory, with the bobbins and looms taking up a large part of their small house. But the hard work told on Gonzalo's health and he became seriously ill. Young John was the one who nursed his father until his death, and this made a profound impression on him. The family was now destitute, with their meagre store of savings used up during Gonzalo's illness. Catalina set off with her three sons to try and persuade the Yepes family to help her. One of the uncles did take in Francis, the eldest son, but when Catalina found that the aunt was mistreating him, she insisted on taking him back home. Then a further tragedy struck, when Luis, the second son, died of malnutrition.

Eventually, in 1551, the remaining three members of the family settled in Medina del Campo, a busy town where Catalina hoped they could make enough of a living to keep the four of them. John was now nine years old, and his mother enrolled him in a school for poor and orphaned children. He learned to read and write in just a few days. The children there were also introduced to some sort of trade, and here he was less successful. He had no aptitude for carpentry, painting, tailoring or any of the other trades on offer, so he had probably not been much use to his mother and father at the loom, either!

John served as an altar boy at the convent of the Augustinian nuns, and when he was about twelve years old he came to the notice of Don Alonzo, the administrator of a local hospital popularly known as Las Bubas. He had seen John serving on the altar, and was impressed with his maturity; all the upheavals and hardships he had already experienced in his young life had made him grow up beyond his years. Don Alonzo offered John a post in the hospital, and he jumped at the chance. His years of caring for his father during his illness had shown that he had a real aptitude for nursing the sick, and this was proved by his work at the hospital. Ostensibly a hospital for those with contagious diseases, most of the patients were actually suffering from sexually-transmitted diseases, due to the number of prostitutes attracted to the town by the many fairs and trading opportunities it afforded.

Hospital job

Faced with the open wounds and ulcers that he dressed, John had to overcome his revulsion, seeing the human being behind the suffering. He not only helped to feed the patients and tend to their physical needs, but he saw to their spiritual and human needs, too. He tried to be a cheerful presence to those who were sad, sat with those who had no relatives to visit them, stayed and prayed with the dying. Still a teenager, people were amazed at the sensitivity, tenderness and compassion with which he went about his tasks.

A task he found perhaps the hardest of all was to go into the streets to beg for alms and donations in kind for the hospital. Poor as his family were, they never had to resort to begging in the street, but John overcame his reluctance for love of his patients.

The work was hard and unrelenting, and already John was experiencing the need for solitude, the need for inner space. At night, he slept in a corner on a bed of twigs and branches. Then he found a bug-infested loft within the hospital grounds where he could be alone and also carry on with his studies in between his work. Don Alonzo had been observing his progress and offered to fund his studies at a newly founded Jesuit school. The priests there soon recognised his ability and his deepening spirituality, and gave him a thorough grounding in Latin and the Spanish classics which would make him eligible to progress to the priesthood.

Carmelite monastery

Those hours of solitude were filled, not only with study, but also with a deepening awareness of the presence of God. When he was twenty-one, Don Alonzo approached John with a further offer. He would fund his studies for the priesthood, and then make him chaplain of Las Bubas. It was a tempting offer. He would be a priest, caring for the sick for whom he felt such compassion, and bringing them even deeper spiritual comfort. It would also mean he could provide better for his mother and brother. The fact that it was a hard decision not to accept the offer made his next move more understandable. Without telling Don Alonzo, he left the hospital on 24th February 1563 and went to the newly founded Carmelite Monastery, where, as could be done at that time, he was immediately admitted, given the tonsure and clothed with the habit. He was given the name of John of Saint Matthias.

If any part of his life could be said to fit the description of being severe and uncompromising, it would be this early part of his Carmelite life. He set himself to follow the Carmelite rule, its fasts, abstinences, all-night vigils, with the utmost rigour. He also loved solitude, and all this didn't endear him to his fellow friars, who considered him too extreme. This impression continued after his Profession the following year, when he was sent to Salamanca to continue his studies.

It was a strange year for him. On the one hand, his studies in Spanish literature opened up to him poetry and the beauty of the Castilian language. He revelled in the richness of life around him, in this bustling, colourful University City where students from all over Spain came to study, and the opportunities it gave to his enquiring mind, always open to the variety of human experience. On the other hand, he lived his Carmelite life with the utmost strictness, having received permission to follow the Primitive Rule. His cell was small and dark, with the minimum of furnishings, but which opened on to the chapel. He could therefore study in the presence of the Blessed Sacrament, and pray into the night. His fellow Carmelites thought him aloof and too serious, and he did not endear himself to them when he was made prefect of

Teresa, who was fifty-two at the time, came to the parlour, she saw a young man of twenty-five, with a swarthy complexion, going prematurely bald; a small man only five feet, two inches. After speaking to him at length, Teresa came out from the parlour exclaiming that she now had a friar and a half - presumably because of John's small stature. But she had also recognised his spiritual stature and knew that her 'little Seneca', as she called him, because of his learning and seriousness, was the one for her.

John was just as delighted, and had no thoughts now of becoming a Carthusian. They agreed that Teresa would look for a suitable house, and John's only stipulation was that he would not have to wait too long. It was several months before she returned to Medina del Campo, and in the meantime had found a small house for them in Duruelo. Fr Antony, who would be the prior, and John, were not deterred by her description of what was barely a hovel, and set off for Duruelo in September 1568, meeting up with a young lay brother who was to join them. They were clad in the robes made for them by Teresa and her nuns, coarser than the robes of the Mitigated friars, and less voluminous.

A first monastery

The house that would become the first monastery of the Reform was barely more than a filthy and ramshackle barn, but the three of them set to with a will to make it habitable. Despite John not having shone at carpentry when at the poor school, he liked working with his hands and proved very useful in his new role of workman. The house consisted of a porch, a small kitchen, a double room and a loft. They made the porch into a church, the loft into the choir where they chanted the Office; the rest composed their primitive living quarters.

John erected a large cross in front of their monastery - and many everywhere else! - so that everyone would know the house was now a religious house. When Teresa visited them some months later she was impressed by what they had achieved. She went round murmuring, 'So many crosses, so many skulls!' This was said with some reservations that the three friars were overdoing the austerity somewhat. Meeting Fr Antony sweeping outside the house with a broad smile on his face, Teresa exclaimed, 'What's this, my Father; what has become of your honour!' 'I curse the day I had any,' he replied.

The monastery was formally consecrated on 28th November 1568, and the friars took new vows as Discalced Carmelites - so called because at that time they went barefoot - joined by two new brothers. John changed his name and would henceforth be known as John of the Cross.

In love with God

He was in his element, whether working in the fields, praying in the tiny choir loft, or walking to the various hamlets around to celebrate Mass and preach to the people. Being one of them, he loved the poor and had no desire ever to put himself above them. His mother, his brother Francis and his wife Anne came to live nearby, all of them helping out in the monastery, cooking the meals and doing the cleaning. Francis would often go with John when he went to the surrounding villages. The two of them would pack some bread for themselves to eat, for John would never accept anything from the people, not wanting to be seen as being paid for his services.

What could the Doctor of the Dark Night, this bookish theologian, have to say that would be meaningful to these poor, hardworking peasants? John was a man in love with God, and who wanted everyone to share in that love in whatever way they could. Throughout his life he had the ability to reach out to every type and class of people. He would later write of the spiritual espousals of the highest union a soul could reach in this life with God. For these working people now he reminded them that they were already united to God by their baptism. That everything in their life, its hardships, its sorrows, and also every joy and expression of love could bring them closer to the God who loved them so much that he had come to be one of them. That everything they did in their lives could be an expression of their love for God.

Growing numbers

The tiny monastery at Duruelo soon proved too small for their growing numbers, and a year later they moved to Pastrana where John helped set up a novitiate. John was shortly sent to help out at some other houses, but had to return to Pastrana a couple of years later to sort out the mess being caused by the novice master there. Fr Angel was making the novices do silly penances, imposing a harsh regime on them, making them a laughing stock in the town and driving away vocations. John had no regard for such behaviour and with his moderation and tact in dealing with others, put a stop to extravagant penances and mortifications. He was no friend of practices that could become ends in themselves. Although he was austere in his own life, in one sense it was not austere to him, as he had always known only that way of life.

Chaplain at the Incarnation

In 1571, Teresa returned to the convent of the Incarnation that had been her home for thirty five years, and that she had left ten years previously to found the monasteries of the Reform. The Apostolic Commissioner, Fr Peter Fernandez, had appointed her Prioress to sort out the chaotic conditions there. Many of the nuns did not have a vocation, having been placed there by their families, and had no intention of giving up their worldly ways. Many were so poor they had hardly anything to eat and had to obtain what they needed from friends and relatives or spend periods of time with them outside the cloister.

When she arrived at the monastery Teresa was met by screaming nuns who barred the door to her. They were afraid she would impose the stricter Rule of the Discalced on them and resented that she had been appointed Prioress over their heads. Eventually a few voices were raised in her support, and they at last prevailed. Once she was able to enter the cloister, Teresa disarmed their hostility by making for the Choir and placing a statue of Our Lady in the Prioress's stall, while she sat on the floor. She then proceeded, with her customary good sense, organising ability and motherly care for the nuns, to bring some order to the convent. She realised, though, that the nuns were in urgent need of good spiritual direction, and therefore obtained permission from Fr Peter for John of the Cross to come as Confessor to the convent.

Reputation as a spiritual director

She recognised his holiness and deep spirituality, while admitting that sometimes he annoyed her - probably because on occasion he disagreed with her! Again, many of the nuns had heard of his reputation for austerity, and feared that he would impose his own strict standards on them. In some ways Teresa could agree with them, as she showed when, a short while after he arrived, she arranged a light-hearted 'contest', styled on the university contests of the time, though with a serious intent. Following a 'word' she heard in prayer, 'Seek yourself in me', she challenged her nuns and priest friends to write an explanation of these words, and she would comment, wittily and caustically, on the results.

Responding to John's offering, she thanked him 'for having explained so well what we did not ask.' and went on:

In his answer he presents very good doctrine for anyone who might want to follow the exercises they make in the Society of Jesus, but not for what we have in mind. Seeking God would be very costly if we could not do so until we were dead to the world. The Magdalene was not dead to the world when she found him, nor was the Samaritan woman or the Canaanite woman. Furthermore, he treats a great deal about becoming one with God in union. But when this union comes about and God grants the soul this favour, one would not say that the soul seeks Him, but that it has already found Him.

There is some truth in Teresa's critique, but not completely. John was gaining an increasing reputation as a spiritual director and guide for people from all walks of life, and with his great sensitivity he recognised that every person, granted their initial union with God in baptism, was unique in their relation with God, as his beloved child; that no one method suited everyone. He was able to adapt his advice and direction to their particular circumstances and to how far advanced they were in the spiritual life. He knew that no-one could attain perfection in one leap, that it was a journey that would last the whole of life. Indeed, he said, to think one could become a saint in a day was a form of spiritual pride.

Nevertheless, when he said, for example, that a bird was just as tethered by a thread as by a thick rope, it could be deeply depressing for someone on the very first rung of the spiritual journey. With all that attached them to material things, they might think it was impossible to unravel all the strands of the rope if even one strand could hold them back, and give up the attempt. But John saw it from a different perspective. He was a man on fire with love for God, and wanted to set others free from everything that held them back from experiencing that love for themselves. For him, the real sadness was to see a soul tethered and caged by their attachment to things, rather than enjoying the glorious liberty of the children of God, for which they had been created.

Helping the nuns of the Incarnation

He wanted to start them off on the first step of that journey. At first, he said, God treats the person as a babe in Christ. He 'nurtures and caresses the soul…like a loving mother who warms her child with the heat of her bosom, nurses it with good milk and tender food, and carries and caresses it in her arms.' At this stage they needed aids to prayer, holy pictures, and methods of prayer that would kindle their love for God.

He recognised that it was no use taking away from a sister a holy picture, a desire for approval, a favourite possession, for example, if she still clung to it. The tether was not in the thing desired, but in the desire for it. He therefore sought to share with the sisters the most desirable thing they could strive for, the love and grace of

God in their hearts, so that they could enjoy the good gifts of God but not be imprisoned by them. He shared with them his own burning love for his Beloved, Jesus, who was all he desired. Once they truly possessed Jesus, then they possessed everything else. As John could rapturously exclaim:

Mine are the heavens and mine is the earth. Mine are the nations, the just are mine, and mine the sinners. The angels are mine, and the Mother of God, and all things are mine, and God Himself is mine and for me, because Christ is mine and all for me.

In this way he gradually encouraged the nuns at the Incarnation to live a more prayerful life. Although not all the nuns were won over by John and Teresa, within a couple of years such order and fervour had been restored that Fr Peter was highly satisfied by the progress made.

Resentments and accusations

With John came another friar, Fr Germán, and at first they stayed at the Calced Carmelite house a few minutes away. However, they met with increasing hostility, as the Calced resented their position with the nuns being taken away. So, the following year they moved into a hut among a small community of builders and workmen living near the monastery. John was in his element, being with the poor he loved so much. He played with the children, taught them their catechism, and for years after the people remembered with affection the kind and sensitive little friar who had lived among them as one of them.

There were a few awkward incidents. He was alone one evening eating his supper when there was a knock on the door and an extremely attractive young woman stood there. She declared that she was madly in love with him and wanted him to know it. John gently invited her in to talk with her, and years later confessed to a friar friend that he had been attracted to her in his turn. But he tactfully and calmly explained to the young woman that his first love was for God, and nothing could take that first place.

There was another young woman who was not living a very good life and who was eventually persuaded by her friends to talk things over with Fr John and make her confession.

Just as he had tended the patients at Las Bubas without judging them, neither did he turn away people such as these with harsh words. God loved them enough to die for them, so by his gentleness and love John tried to give them an experience of God's love for them, that would encourage them in their turn to draw nearer to Him.

Years later, he was confronted by yet another young woman with a young baby in her arms, who declared that he was the father. Gently, John asked when the baby was conceived, and pointed that he was in a completely different part of Spain at the time and therefore could not possibly be the child's father. Yet again, he showed his kindliness, and liked to share the joke with his friars.

His attempts were not always appreciated. He was attacked and beaten up by a man who was having a relationship with one of the nuns at the Incarnation convent, who resented the influence John was having on her by drawing her away from her attachment to the man. John refused to name the man who had attacked him.

At Avila, John lived his quiet life, ministering to the nuns, the families and those who sought his advice and counsel, but further afield there was growing tension between the Calced and Discalced as Teresa founded more monasteries that grew in popularity. There were good and holy and well-meaning people on both sides, but inevitably jealousy and fear. Also, permission to make these new monastic foundations came from different sources in the hierarchy which caused conflict as to who had the authority. There were misunderstandings on both sides, often innocently: when, for example, Teresa did not receive in time a letter from the Superior General, Fr Rubeo, who then interpreted her non-compliance as rebellion and disobedience. John himself was deeply hurt and worried by these conflicts, and it was affecting his health.

Immediate danger

Matters came to a head in 1577, when the Calced friars decided to take matters into their own hands. They saw John as one of the ringleaders of the disobedient Discalced friars and also, because of his spiritual stature, as the main problem. If they could remove him from the scene, then perhaps the whole Reform would collapse. In Calced eyes, he had disobeyed the orders of the Superior General to rein back his activity, and continued to support Teresa, whereas in John's eyes he was under obedience to the higher authority of the Papal Nuncio. Things could not continue as they were, and in December 1577, the Calced friars decided to kidnap him.

Toledo Prison

On a bitterly cold night, 3rd December 1577, just as John and Germán were praying together before retiring, a group of friars burst in and seized them, then rough-handled them up to their monastery. They were forced to take off the rough habit of the Reform and put on the softer habit of the Calced. Then they were put in cells. When John was let out to say Mass, he used the opportunity to escape back to their hut to burn documents that he did not want to fall into the hands of the Calced; he just managed to do so before he was seized again. To prevent another escape, Fr Germán was taken to a monastery of San Pablo de la Moraleja, from where he managed to escape a couple of weeks later, and John was taken, blindfolded and bound, to Toledo.

Deprivations

His prison for the next nine months was a tiny cell, six foot by ten, with a slit a few inches wide, high up in the wall letting on to a corridor as the only light. To say his Office - his breviary was the only book allowed him - he had to stand on a stool and read it in the short while that the sun passed through it. The cell was a sort of closet leading off from a guest room, and was near the monastery toilets, so the smell was noisome. John had only a bucket for his own use, and was not allowed to change his clothes, a hard trial for one who, contrary to the custom of the time, kept himself very clean. It was freezing cold in the frigid Toledan winter and unbearably hot and stifling in the summer.

Every Friday, he was brought out from his cell to eat bread and water on the floor of the refectory, as the friars ate their dinner. Then he was harangued by the Prior, who accused him of disobedience, of disregarding the commands of the Superior General and of trying to destroy the Order. The friars then went one by one to whip him until his back bled. He was then led back to his cell. His health was already frail and suffered even more under such treatment.

Trials

Friars would stand outside his door, saying that everyone else had given up the Reform, and only he was proving obdurate. The darkness and the accusations began to seep into his soul. Was he truly disobedient when he thought he was following the permissions of his superiors? John was not to know how worried his friends were. They did not know where he was or what had happened to him. He did not know that Teresa was sending off letters to those who had any power and influence, from the King downwards, to try and obtain his release. She feared for his life, saying that he would have been better off being seized by the Moors. John, too, feared for his life, as he heard the friars whispering he would never get out alive. When he was served with a rare delicacy of sardines, he could hardly force himself to eat them, thinking they had been poisoned. He became weaker, even more frail, and paranoid. They even tried bribery: once with, of all things, a golden rosary, and then with the post of Prior in a Calced monastery.

In his *The Dark Night* written later, he was surely drawing on his own experience of this time, describing 'the spiritual darkness in which he is engulfed and which afflict him with doubts and fears... Nevertheless, in the midst of these dark and loving afflictions, the soul feels the presence of someone and an interior strength which so fortifies and accompanies it that when this weight of anxious darkness passes, it often feels alone, empty and weak.'

Interior darkness

But even this sense of 'a presence of someone' was taken away from him. He had no sense of God, was unable to pray, and knew only utter silence and emptiness. He was being stripped down to the very essence of his being and he felt that he could very easily die. Gradually, though, by May he began to gather once again the strength that enabled him to claw his way back up out of his interior darkness. In the darkness of his prison sometimes the only sound he could hear was the river Tagus running below the monastery. And gradually the sound of the water took on the dimensions of the Blessed Trinity flowing within him:

For I know well the spring that flows and runs,
Although it is night.

Coming from an unknown source, hidden and yet known, the streams of the Trinity were watering his soul. These were a light in the darkness, a living spring, even the bread of life, (as he expressed it in the poem) when he was not allowed to say Mass and was being denied Holy Communion.

His conditions were somewhat eased at that time when a different friar, John of Saint Mary was set to guard him. Brother John was appalled at the community's treatment of him, and was deeply impressed by his prisoner's gentleness, patience and kindness, even in the midst of such appalling trials, and began to help as much as he could. While the other friars had their siestas in the afternoon, John let him out so that he could walk in the guest room and gave him a clean tunic. He also brought John pen, paper and ink. John folded the sheets carefully into a little book, and began to pen some of the most exquisite poetry in the Spanish language.

Writings from intense suffering

In the fetid darkness of his prison, from the depths of his spiritual darkness, John began to picture the beautiful Spanish countryside that he loved so much and which never failed to raise his soul to the beauty of the God who had created such loveliness. He recalled the words of his favourite book of the Bible, the Song of Songs. He drew on his love of Spanish poetry to express his burning love for God and his search for him in the darkness.

> Where have you hidden,
> Beloved, and left me moaning?
> You fled like the stag
> After wounding me;
> I went out calling you, and you were gone.
>
> Seeking my Love
> I will head for the mountains and for watersides,
> I will not gather flowers,
> Nor fear wild beasts,
> I will go beyond strong men and frontiers.

Escape

As his spirit began to grow stronger, his body began to weaken even further, and he knew he had to escape or die. He had to get beyond the 'strong men' who imprisoned him, and the 'frontier' of his prison cell. Matters came to a head the day before the Feast of the Assumption (15th August), when the Prior paid an unexpected visit to his cell. John asked him if he could celebrate Mass for the Feast of the Assumption, but the Prior stormed out of the cell contemptuously - 'Over my dead body!' John knew he meant it. It was now or never.

Already on his walks outside his cell John had begun to take his bearings and to see if there was any way of escape. The guest room overlooked a wall some twelve feet below its window, with the River Tagus flowing beyond rocky cliffs. Taking some thread Brother John had given him to mend his habit, he weighted the end and assessed the drop. Every day he began to loosen the screws of his cell door. His prison cell was far enough from the cells of the other friars so they would not hear the bolts falling on the ground.

John planned his escape for that night. After the Prior had left, he tore his blankets into strips that should reach down to the wall and waited anxiously for the night. But unexpected obstacles arose. A couple of friars arrived and were put into the guest room, blocking John's escape route. But he was determined to go ahead with his plan. He waited until the two men were asleep, then at about two in the morning he carefully forced the lock on to the ground. The noise disturbed the friars, but John held his breath and waited until they groggily returned to sleep. Creeping past them with the knotted blankets and his precious poems, he cautiously tied his makeshift rope to the wooden balcony. The wall twelve feet below him was barely two feet in width; one slip, and he could be dashed on the cliff rocks below into the Tagus.

He made it safely, landing on the wall and walked cautiously along it for a while until he thought it safe enough to reach ground level. Unfortunately, he realised he had jumped into the garden of a convent of nuns. If he was found in such a compromising place, further imprisonment would be even more dire! Summoning up his last reserves of strength he hauled himself back on to the wall and walked along it until he reached a street. He then had to pass by the blandishments of a prostitute and the drunken ribaldry of a couple of revellers, before he finally found his way to the convent of Discalced nuns. They were not yet awake, so he huddled in the courtyard of a nearby house until the rising bell began to toll.

John went to the convent door. 'Daughter, I am Fr John of the Cross,' he said to the startled portress. 'I have just escaped from prison. Please tell your Prioress I'm here.' Mother Anne of the Angels rushed and saw the little friar, exhausted and bedraggled, and quickly let him in. A sick sister had asked to go to confession; John was a priest, so he could come in to hear her confession. They then looked after him, gave him food and clean clothes. By this time the friars had realised he escaped and came to the convent looking for him. With admirable aplomb and circumlocution the portress was able to deny his whereabouts without actually lying.

Mother Anne realised John could not stay in the convent, so she contacted Don Peter, the nearby hospital administrator. He came to collect John, dressed in a cassock, and took him secretly to the hospital where he could rest and recuperate. His ordeal was over.

Ascent of Mount Carmel

The difficulties between Calced and Discalced rumbled on, so in October the Discalced held a Chapter. When the Papal Legate heard of it, he excommunicated everyone who had taken part, and in response the Discalced sent two friars to Rome to request the separation of the two branches of the Carmelite Order. The Chapter also appointed John of the Cross as temporary Superior of the Pastrana monastery, El Calvario, while the Prior was away in Rome. The journey from the north of Spain to Andalusia in the south would have been arduous for someone in good health, and even more so for John in his emaciated and weakened state, so the good Don Peter sent two of his men to accompany him.

'A divine, heavenly man'

They broke their journey at the convent at Beas that Teresa had founded three years earlier, so that John could rest for a few days. The visit was not a success. Gaunt and exhausted, he was withdrawn, a shadow of his former self. He then shocked the Prioress, Mother Anne of Jesus, by daring to call the great Teresa, *La Madre*, his daughter! Anne wrote a letter of complaint to Teresa, and asked that she send them a real spiritual director instead of such an insignificant little friar. From Avila, Teresa wrote in return:

I am really shocked, daughter, that you should be complaining like this without the least reason, when you have among you Fr John of the Cross. He is a divine, heavenly man. I assure you, my daughter, since he left us I have not found another like him in the whole of Castile, nor anyone else who inspires the soul with such fervour to journey to Heaven. You would never believe how lonely I feel without him. Consider what a great treasure you have in that saint, and see that all the sisters in your house talk to him and tell them about their souls. They will see what good it does them and will find themselves in every way greatly advanced in spirituality and perfection, for Our Lord has given him special grace for that purpose.

I can assure you I should be glad if I had my Fr John of the Cross here, for he is indeed the Father of my soul and one of those with whom it does me most good to have converse. Treat him with complete frankness, my daughter, for, I assure you, you can behave with him just as you would with me and he will satisfy you fully in your needs, for he is very spiritual and has great experience and learning. He is sorely missed here by those who were brought up on his teaching. So give thanks to God for having ordained that you should have him so near you. I am writing to tell him to attend to your wants, and he is so kind that I know he will do so whenever any need presents itself.

Superior of Pastrana monastery

In Pastrana, some of the friars were awaiting his arrival with trepidation. They had been novices with him in Salamanca, and were wondering whether his austerity and rigidity of that time had been made even harsher by his prison experience. As always, he confounded their expectations. He found a community living very simply and frugally, in lovely surroundings which revived his spirits and gave him the simple living he loved. He soon won over the friars by his gentleness and kindness.

Every Saturday he would travel over to Beas to hear the nuns' confessions and give them talks and spiritual direction, besides helping them in the garden. Mother Anne of Jesus soon revised her poor impression of him and became one of his staunchest supporters and dearest daughter. He shared with them the poems he had written in prison, which he had set to popular tunes; they were soon circulating round the convents so that the sisters could sing and dance to them. The Beas nuns also began to ask him to explain them, and spurred on by their interest he began to write two of his greatest works, *The Ascent of Mount Carmel* and *The Spiritual Canticle*.

Understanding John's writings

For many, John of the Cross's works are not easy reading. His works can seem too formal in places; in others he soars to such heights that few feel it could possibly apply to them. But John himself gives us some hints as to how to approach his works.

As with the Beas nuns, his poems are a good place to start. John said that his commentaries were what he himself drew from them, but others might get different insights. So we can start by reading them, pondering on them, letting them speak personally to the heart. John has such a richness of language and vivid imagery that one can take even a single word and let it sink deeply into the soul, before going to the commentary itself.

In his works, although John rarely speaks directly of himself, in fact he is writing from his own experience, baring his very soul. As John puts it, they 'were obviously composed with a certain burning love of God'. He also wrote from what he was learning from others as they came to him for spiritual guidance. He was a good listener. As Sr Frances remarked, 'He was so holy it seemed as if every word we spoke to him opened a door for him.' She herself gave an example of this when he asked her how she prayed, and she said, 'By gazing on God's beauty, and rejoicing that he has it.'

This reply made such an impression on John that later he sang of this rejoicing in God's beauty:

Let us so act that by means of this loving activity we may attain to the vision of ourselves in Your beauty in eternal life. That is: That I be so transformed in Your beauty that we may be alike in beauty, and both behold ourselves in Your beauty, possessing now Your very beauty; this, in such a way that each looking at the other may see in the other his own beauty, since both are Your beauty alone, I being absorbed in Your beauty; hence, I shall see myself You in Your beauty, and You shall see me in Your beauty; that I may resemble You in Your beauty and Your beauty be Your beauty; wherefore I shall be You in Your beauty, and You will be me in Your beauty, because Your very beauty will be my beauty; and therefore we shall behold each other in Your beauty.

Because he was drawing on such a wide pool of experience, John knew that not everything he wrote would apply to everyone. It is a question of finding that word, that phrase, that passage in his writings that speaks individually to our particular circumstances. John was fond of writing out little 'maxims' for the sisters, many of which were collected and preserved. So in a similar way it might be helpful to write out, or highlight those passages for prayer and meditation that strike one most.[1]

John rooted in scripture

John of the Cross was steeped in the Bible and knew it by heart. His students said that when he gave a lecture he had only the Bible in front of him for reference. Simply put, in his lectures and his writings what he was doing was explaining the Scriptures. If he seems radical and uncompromising, then it is no less radical than the call of Jesus to leave everything and follow him, that anyone who was not ready to give up everything for the sake of the Kingdom of Heaven was not worthy of him. From Saint Paul, saying he was treating his converts like children, giving them milk, to Jesus' call to take up our cross, to follow the narrow way, to the glorious life that is the Christian vocation, John is all Scripture. If that life seems more than we can imagine, then it is just what the scriptures tell us is our destiny. We are called to be children of God, sharing in the divine nature, the dwelling place of the Trinity, life, a foretaste of which we can have even in this life, far beyond anything we could ask or imagine.

What is the 'Ascent'?

John also drew for the nuns of Beas his famous sketch of the Ascent of Mount Carmel.

There are three paths going up the mountain - to the left, the goods of heaven, on the right, the goods of earth, both given as possessions, joy, knowledge, consolation, rest. A narrow pathway goes up between these two paths - the path of Mount Carmel, the perfect spirit - nothing, nothing, nothing, and even on the Mount nothing.

Dark nights

This can be very daunting - what does 'nothing' mean? Does it mean going through such a terrible stripping, inwardly and outwardly, as John himself experienced in his Toledo prison? John's experience was extreme, but in lesser ways all of us have trials and the stresses of life - the cold of winter, the heat of summer, a crowded train, and the frustration of a traffic jam. We all have to give and take in family life, at work, in the supermarket. Then there are the tensions with friends and family, the unkind word, the gossip. We want to do God's will, but are we really doing it? Are we deceiving ourselves, when others are telling us we are wrong? We can feel confused, angry, out of our depth. These occasions, 'nights', are all opportunities to cling to God, even when he does not seem to be there, to say yes to God, to others, and no to self. John says that there are passive nights and active nights. The passive nights are those circumstances in our life, in our prayer, permitted or willed by God. The active nights are those things we do for ourselves, to deny our own wills, to put ourselves out for others, to actively hold ourselves in prayer, content to allow God to work in us.

John says that it is '*nada*', nothing, along the narrow route to the summit, because he is a man in love, and he wants to choose the swiftest way to the one he loves. He is like the merchant who sells all that he has to purchase the pearl of great price, and he wants us to follow in his steps. Like Saint Paul, he considers everything as loss compared with the supreme good of knowing Christ Jesus his Lord, and to gain him. Like Saint Paul again, he knows that nothing can separate him from the love of God in Christ Jesus.

John writes that [in order] 'to come to possess all' we should 'desire the possession of nothing'. He is saying that our self-denial has an aim, a goal. It is not an end in itself. He is saying that all the gifts of heaven and earth, which are gifts to us from God himself, and therefore good, are not God. If we seek those goods for themselves then we are seeking something less than God. We will not be satisfied, for only God himself can satisfy hearts that he has made for himself.

There comes a time when prayer becomes dry and empty, boring, and the helps to prayer that we have relied on no longer satisfy. Then, John says, we have to go with that dryness, that darkness, at God's own pace, content to rest in that silence and emptiness. We must be content to 'know without knowing'.

At this time God is desiring to increase our capacity to receive him, for we have infinite capacity for God; so often we limit him; as John wrote tersely to Sister Anne of Saint Albert, 'It seems you want to measure God by the measure of your own capacity, but it will not be so.' Since love is the motive, the way and the goal, how can we limit love? John puts the highest ideal before us, because he has such a profound understanding of what we are capable of and what we were created for:

> Oh then, soul, most beautiful among all creatures, so anxious to know the dwelling place of your Beloved, that you may go in quest of Him and be united with Him, now we are telling you that you yourself are His dwelling and His secret chamber and hiding place.

John had an interesting correspondence with the nuns at the newly founded convent of Córdoba. They were surrounded by building works; some of the nuns had come from other convents and felt lonely; and they were all finding their way in new surroundings. These humdrum circumstances John says, are 'dark nights' in which they can advance in their life of union with God: 'His Majesty has done this in order to bring you greater profit. The more He wants to give, the more He makes us desire - even to the point of leaving us empty in order to fill us with goods.' This poverty of spirit is liberating: 'he who is poor in spirit is happier and more constant in the midst of want, because he has placed his all in his nothingness, and in all things he thus finds freedom of heart. O happy nothingness, and happy hiding place of the heart! For the heart has such power that it subjects all things to itself; this it does by desiring to be subject to nothing and losing all care so as to burn the more in love.'

Complete freedom

John says that we are not alone in this journey up the Mount and attain God only at the end of the journey, because he surrounds the whole of the mountain with the gifts and fruits of the Holy Spirit - peace, joy, happiness, delight, wisdom, justice, fortitude, charity, piety. In the words of Saint Catherine of Siena, 'All the way to heaven is heaven, because Jesus said "I am the Way"'. The goal of the journey is to live in the freedom of the law of love, to live for the glory and honour of God. Triumphantly he proclaims: 'Here there is no longer any way, because for the just man there is no law, he is a law unto himself. In the words of Saint Augustine - 'love and do what you will'. It is the freedom of Saint Paul who said that he knew how to be rich and how to go without, having the strength given him by Christ for every circumstance.

Prior and Traveller

John was in Pastrana for only eight months when he was called to new pastures. The Discalced were continuing to grow, and it was decided to found a monastery in Baeza, which would also be their first House of Studies. There was a university nearby that the young friars could attend. They appointed John as the founding rector, and on 13 June 1579, he set out with three friars from Pastrana for Baeza.

A true father to his friars

The monastery was founded in poverty - John refused the offer of mattresses for his friars - but he ensured it was a happy and fervent foundation. As Prior, he shared in all the household tasks, sweeping, cleaning, choosing the simplest and poorest room for his cell and doing repairs and alterations that were needed in the new foundation. He looked after his friars with a deep humanity that was sometimes lacking at that time. There was a rule that the Prior should go round the cells to make sure the friars were obeying the rules. John did so - but rattled his rosary loudly so they knew he was coming.

If he saw that a brother was troubled or sad, he would walk with him in the garden, talking with him until he was at peace and happy again. Nevertheless, if he discerned that the brother was going through a period of dryness that was not of his own making, he would encourage him to embrace the darkness and the dryness, the lack of spiritual satisfaction, and find his joy in embracing the will of God, regardless of his own feelings; to be happy in the understanding that God was giving Himself to the soul in that darkness in a far greater and deeper degree than could be measured by feelings of sweetness and pleasure.

For himself, he felt intensely lonely. In a letter to Mother Catalina de Jesus he likened himself to Jonah being swallowed up by a whale and vomited up on an alien port - 'you are not as abandoned and alone as I am down here.' Like Teresa, he could not abide the Andalusians - so even saints have their likes and dislikes! However, he accepted his situation with his usual abandonment to the will of God - 'after all, abandonment is a file and the endurance of darkness leads to great light. May it please God that we do not walk in darkness!'

John loved nature, and although he was homesick for his native Castile, he revelled in the Andalusian countryside and often used to take the brothers out for picnics where they could relax, pray and refresh their spirits in the beauty that to him were the scattering of God's graces as he passed. It was not so much, now, that the beauty of creation lifted his soul to God, but that creation was so imbued with God's beauty that he saw everything in God. He often went out by himself, sometimes for days at a time, away from the bustle of the city, to renew his spirit. Night for him had a special meaning, so happy was he with the spiritual equivalent of the darkness. He would often go out into the dark to pray, or lean out of his cell window, drinking in the night sky. In a beautiful passage, he gives some inkling of his thoughts as he prayed in the night air:

> In that nocturnal tranquillity and silence and in that knowledge of the divine light the soul becomes aware of Wisdom's wonderful harmony and sequence in the variety of His creatures and works. Each of them is endowed with a certain likeness of God and in its own way gives voice to what God is in it. So creatures will be for the soul a harmonious symphony of sublime music surpassing all concerts and melodies of the world.

The friars loved the evening recreations, when they relaxed and conversed. John carved small wooden figures or wove wicker baskets. He filled them with such joy with his conversation that often the brothers who were serving the community supper, and would therefore eat after the others, would forgo their supper so as not to miss anything.

Community life, care for the sick

For John, the community was contemplative first, and prayer took priority, with their apostolate flowing from their prayer life. Their apostolate to the poor was needed the year after their arrival when a flu epidemic hit the town. John always had a deep concern for the sick, and his training in Las Bubas years before stood him in good stead now. He was tireless in looking after whole families, nursing them, cooking, feeding, changing their clothes, and by his very presence bringing comfort and hope to them. Sadly, his mother, who was living in Medina del Campo, caught the flu and died. As she was so closely linked to the Carmelite nuns there, she was buried in their cemetery.

When any of his friars became sick, no matter how poor his community was, John always made sure that the brother had all the medicines and care that he needed. He would spend hours by the sick bed, and this concern for the brothers under his care made him deeply loved.

He was also much in demand at the university for his spiritual direction and guidance, as well as in the town itself. People flocked to him, and as well he took part in the academic life of the university, taking part in disputations, arranging the course of study for his students. In addition, he was continuing to write *The*

Ascent of Mount Carmel (which was never finished), and *The Spiritual Canticle*. Being so scholastic himself, he loved the university atmosphere.

More responsibilities with new Order

As if all this was not enough, he was also much involved with developments in the Order. In 1580, the Discalced were finally set up as a separate Province from the Calced. The first legal Chapter took place on 3rd March 1581, and John was elected as one of the definitors or advisors on to the Governing Body. This involved him in much administrative work, and a great deal of travelling, visiting the various foundations and setting up new ones. The mystic, poet and lover, author of some of the greatest spiritual works of the Christian Church, did not live in an ivory tower, but plunged into the most mundane tasks and administration, with all the headaches that these involved.

John was Prior at Baeza for two years, and was then appointed Prior to the Granada foundation of Los Martires. He arrived on 20th January and found the house in a poor state. He was even forced to beg for bread for the brothers. The building was still being constructed, so John rolled up his sleeves and joined in, designing various extra parts of the monastery such as an extra cloister.

Isolation deepens, inner freedom grows

Even further away from his beloved Castile, he felt his isolation deeply, and this was increased when Saint Teresa died on 15th October later that year. The last time he had seen her had been the previous November, and it does not seem to have been a happy parting. As the first snows fell, John had made the gruelling journey from Granada to Avila, where Teresa was at the time, to bring her and a few nuns back with him to found a convent in Granada. Teresa adamantly refused to go, as she had heard an inner locution that she should go to Burgos. John had always been concerned at the weight Teresa gave to her visions and locution, but was unable to sway her. Despite his exhaustion - and Teresa's headache after that tiring session with him - he left the following morning to return to Granada. Anne of Jesus made the foundation and was to prove a staunch friend to him. Nevertheless, John retained a deep affection for Teresa. He kept all her letters to him in a bag that went with him on his travels. Sadly, he felt he was too attached to them and burnt them all. Perhaps their loss was a greater testimony to his character, both loving and uncompromising with himself, than the letters themselves would have been.

In 1584 a famine hit Andalusia, and once again he showed his compassion to all those in need. No one was turned away from the monastery gates, even if the community had little enough for themselves. And he showed his sensitivity when he privately brought food and help to high standing families who were in need, so that they did not lose face, in that class-ridden society, by coming to beg at the monastery gates themselves.

John had reached that state of inner freedom when he could truly be himself and not be forced into a mould of others' making. As Prior and an official in his Order now, he himself had a status that afforded him some dignity, but he refused to be judged by such standards. He might be helping out with building work on a house, or working in the garden in his rough habit. A high ranking official would be brought to him and be greeted by John just as he was. As he said to one visitor who expressed his surprise, 'After all, I am the son of a weaver.' Later on, his brother Francisco was often with him. Francisco remained what he always was, a poor workman, and John would introduce him with great pride as the greatest treasure he had on earth. To John, earthly rank or attainment did not matter. What did matter was that they were all children of God, and as such, deserving of his respect and love, whatever their rank or lack of it..

The Order met for their second Chapter on 1st May 1583 and John was elected 2nd definitor and Vicar Provincial. He was able, between helping the townsfolk during the famine, to write further commentaries that completed his major writings which he first discussed with his Beas nuns, then returned to his monastery to write. He finished *The Spiritual Canticle*, wrote *The Dark Night*. In Granada, he met a noble laywoman, Anne of Peñalosa. She was grieving deeply over the death of her husband, and John was able to guide her spiritual journey. It was for her he wrote *The Living Flame of Love* in fourteen days, in the midst of his hectic administrative duties.

From 1585, for the next three years, he was almost constantly on the road in his role as Vicar Apostolic, attending chapters, visiting the various foundations, founding new convents and friaries. At one such foundation, that of Cordoba, he nearly lost his life. A stone wall that was being built fell on the cell in which he was working, and the workmen scrabbled frantically to dig him out, fearing he was dead. However, they found him crouched in a corner under a statue of Our Lady that had fallen above him, laughing and saying that it was she who had saved him.

To his delight, in 1588 he was appointed prior of the Segovia friary, which meant that he was back in his beloved Castile. A new friary was still being built away from the dampness of the nearby river, so John joined in with the building work, breaking stones to build the walls, carrying materials to the workmen. He also designed and helped build an aqueduct to carry water to the new monastery. He enjoyed the physical work, above all being in the company not only of his brother friars, but also the workmen with whom he always felt an affinity.

To suffer and be despised

Back in Castile he was nearer to his beloved brother who was able to visit him more often. To his brother he revealed an experience he had had. Praying before a picture of Christ carrying his cross one day, he heard an inner voice calling his name, and responded inwardly, 'Here I am.' The voice then asked him what reward he would like for all that he had done and all he had have suffered.' John's response was, 'To suffer and to be looked down upon.' He told this to his brother so that when Francis saw him having trials he would not be distressed, knowing that it was what he had desired and that they were God's will for him.

Major disagreements on role of new Order

At present, the storm clouds were barely on the horizon. Since Nicolas Doria, the Vicar General, was away on a visitation of all the houses of the Reform, John had to fulfil the many administrative duties connected with the Reform. As ever, he was assiduous in spiritual direction of the nuns under his jurisdiction and whoever needed his help.

Storm clouds began to break over him when the Father General, Nicolas Doria, convened an Extraordinary Chapter in June 1590. John had a premonition that things would go badly for him. When one of the Segovian nuns said that she was sure he would return to them as their Provincial, he replied, quietly and with certainty, 'I shall be thrown into a corner like an old rag.'

One source of disagreement went as far back as 1581 at the Chapter at Almodovar del Campo. John had come into conflict with Fr Jerome Gracián who had been a favourite and close collaborator of Saint Teresa. Gracián wanted the friars to be more active in the apostolate, whereas John insisted that they should be primarily contemplative, from which their apostolate would flow. He did not want their contemplative vocation to take second place and perhaps be squeezed out. This tension between the active and contemplative aspects of the Carmelite friar's life had a long history. The Order traces its origins back to the time of the Crusades, when some of the crusaders decided to settle in the Holy Land, on Mount Carmel, where Elijah and Elisha had founded a 'school of prophets', living a life of community and contemplation. Ever since, Carmelites have looked on the two great prophets as their spiritual forebears. When the

Muslims defeated the crusaders and drove them out of the Holy Land, the friars fled to the West, where they took up an active apostolate, sometimes to the detriment of their contemplative base.

Power struggle

At the Madrid Chapter the problem was more a clash of personalities between Gracián, who represented the moderates and Doria who wanted more control. Although Teresa had not taken personally to Doria, a Genoese who had been a banker before entering the Discalced, she had prized Doria's organisational skills, but he was rigid and authoritarian. The younger Gracián had a brilliant mind, a distinguished scholar and organiser, and had a much more pleasing and charming manner, although his impetuosity and rashness made him powerful enemies - including Doria.

Now, Doria put forward some proposals with which John adamantly disagreed. Doria changed the government of the Order, concentrating all power in the hands of a permanent committee. He also wanted to take revenge against the formidable Mother Anne of Jesus, who, supported by John of the Cross, opposed his plans for the nuns and wanted to seek papal approbation for their constitutions. In addition, he wanted to expel Gracián from the Order, seeing him as a dangerous rival to his own power.

John of the Cross had already warned Gracián that this might happen. He had been horrified when Gracián had proposed that Doria should succeed him as Provincial: he was elected by only two votes. Now, he felt that Gracián was being unfairly treated, and said so. Although many of the other friars privately agreed with him, they were too cowed by Doria's dictatorial manner to speak out.

God is always good

What John had foreseen came to pass. Doria saw his prestige and the reverence in which so many held him for his spiritual stature as a threat to his own authority and he left the Chapter a simple friar, stripped of any post. There were even plans to send him to Mexico, although this never materialised. Instead, he was sent to a remote friary at La Peñuela. For John, it was a relief no longer to have all his administrative tasks, and to pursue the life of prayer for which he always yearned, whatever his outward activity over the previous years. As he remarked of those years, when he spent his journeys praying, singing psalms, 'I am well, but my soul lags far behind'.

The letter he wrote to Mother Anne of Jesus shortly after the Chapter shows his state of mind: '[God] has arranged this that we may show it by our actions…this is not evil or harmful, neither for me nor for anyone. It is in my favour since, being freed and relieved from the care of souls, I can, if I want and with God's help, enjoy peace, solitude, and the delightful fruit of forgetfulness of self and of all things'. He made the most of the nature he so loved at Peñuela, going for hours into the countryside to pray and be alone with his Beloved. Even so, he was not out of contact with the many people whom he had directed, and continued to guide them by letter.

Even so, he would not have been human if he had not felt hurt by the antagonism and even hatred of which he had been the butt at the Chapter. As he wrote to Anne of Peñalosa, he liked Peñuela very much: 'The vastness of the desert is a great help to the soul and the body, although the soul fares very poorly. The Lord must desire that it have its spiritual desert.' He described his simple life to her, which suited him so much: 'This morning we have already returned from gathering our chick-peas, and so the mornings go by. On another day we shall thresh them. It is nice to handle these mute creatures, better than being badly handled by living ones.'

Love your enemies

He was also concerned about what was happening to the Order under Doria's authority, and the unhappiness it was causing to the nuns. He wrote to Sr Leonor advising her not to dwell on things, 'because what should be occupied in God be occupied in this... Let the garden be closed, then, without pain or worry, for he who entered bodily for his disciples, when the doors were closed, and gave them peace, without them knowing or imagining that this could be, nor how, will enter in spirit into the soul.. and he will fill her with peace.'

He had need of that peace for himself, because a new definitor, Fr Diego Evangelista, elected at the Madrid Chapter, was given the task of investigating Fr Gracián, with a view to carrying out his expulsion from the Order that Doria had proposed. The nuns at Granada were so worried at the interrogations to which they had been subjected and the way what they said was being twisted and misinterpreted, that they burnt a whole sackful of John's letters and other writings. Hearing of this activity, John was deeply hurt, but refused to say anything against Fr Diego. This campaign continued for the rest of John's life, and hearing of his death, Diego expressed regret that he had not managed to expel him from the Order before he died. The hapless Gracián was not so 'fortunate'. He was expelled, captured and tortured by Barbary pirates, escaped, and, not able to re-enter the Discalced, died as a Calced friar.

Last Days

John of the Cross had said to Mother Anne that his health was good, but that was to change in September of that year, 1591. Bearing in mind his austere life, the sufferings his body had undergone in Toledo, the incessant travels over Spain without the benefit of modern roads, his health had borne up very well. He had a bout of fever a little earlier, and now he went down with another bout, and his right leg became inflamed. He needed medical attention, but Peñuela was so remote that there were no medicines available.

He had to make a decision whether to go to Baeza, where he would be welcomed, but would be surrounded by visitors wanting to see him, or to the recently founded house at Ubeda. He chose Ubeda. It was a twenty mile journey by mule in the torrid heat, and he was almost dead with pain and exhaustion by the time he arrived. It was discovered that he had untreated erysipelas in his foot, a disease of the nerve endings which would break out into painful sores. The doctor had to scrape away the diseased flesh without anaesthetic - with no understanding of sterilisation, that would probably have made the condition worse.

Illness

He was pleased to see Fr Alonzo, who had been one of his novices at Granada, but his welcome from the Prior, Francis Chrysostom, was much less welcome. He resented the drain on his time and resources that a sick friar would mean to the community. In addition, as his Provincial some time before, John had had to reprimand him, and Francis had borne him a grudge ever since. Now he would have his revenge. He gave John a tiny cell that only John, being so small, could enter without stooping. In the encroaching winter, it was bitterly cold, with the wind coming in through cracks in the wall. Sick as John was, the Prior ordered him to attend all the community functions, and publicly reprimanded him when he had to stay in bed. He accused John of using his illness to seek sympathy, what a bad example he was giving, how lax he was in observing the Rule. He refused to allow any of the brothers or any visitors to see him.

Wherever John had been Prior, his attention to the sick was peerless. However poor the community might be, all that the sick might need was given them. Now, Fr Francis refused to provide him with the medicines and food that John needed.

His treatment was scandalising the community, however, and when Fr Francis forbade Fr Bernard, his infirmarian, to look after John any more, this was the last straw for Bernard. He wrote to the Provincial, Fr Antony of Jesus, John's old companion from the Duruelo days, who immediately came to Ubedo, saw the conditions that John was suffering, reprimanded the Prior severely, and made sure that he was given better treatment.

Where there is no love, bring love

John accepted all this without complaint. In July of that year, he had written to Mother Mary of the Incarnation, Prioress of the Segovia convent, who was distressed at the treatment he was receiving: '...do not let what is happening to me, my daughter, cause you any grief, for it does not cause me any... Men do not do these things, but God, who knows what is suitable for us and arranges things for our good. Think nothing else but that God ordains all, and where there is no love, put love, and you will draw out love...' Even more now, when he was being treated with such little love, he responded only with love and forgiveness.

'At the evening of life,' said John of the Cross, 'we will be judged by love.' John was approaching the evening of his life, and love was the meaning of his life. Love was his response to everything. He refused to say an ill word of those who hated him. He received letters telling him of Fr Diego's campaign against him, which were kept in a bag at the bottom of his bed. He ordered them to be burnt, so that they would not damage the Order after his death. He had no word of complaint of his treatment, seeing everything as a permitted by God for his good. Perhaps alluding to the nuns' concerns about Doria's governance, but surely applicable to his own situation, he wrote to Mother Anne of St Albert, 'you already know, daughter, the trials they are now suffering. God permits it to try his elect. In silence and in hope shall our strength be.'

'Have a great love for those who contradict and fail to love you,' he wrote to another nun, 'for in this way love is begotten in a heart that has no love. God so acts with us, for He loves us that we might love by means of the very love He bears toward us.' It worked, because at John's deathbed, the Prior knelt in tears and asked his forgiveness.

Approaching death

If Fr Diego was slow in recognising John's sanctity, others did not. News soon got round that a saint was dying in the Ubeda monastery and many wanted to see him and obtain his blessing. The woman who came daily to collect the bloody and pus-laden bandages to wash and return them, carefully collected them as relics.

By now, the erysipelas had spread to his whole body, causing him agony and discomfort. As a big ulceration in his back caused him great pain to be moved, the brothers rigged up a rope pulley so he could haul himself up. As he helped himself up John quipped, 'At least I am light!' He spoke truly, because there was hardly any flesh left on his emaciated body.

Knowing his love of music - he would often sing hymns and psalms on his travels - the brothers brought along some musicians to play to him, hoping it would take his mind off his pain. After a short while, John requested they be sent away, he was listening to 'the silent music of love' within his soul. In a beautiful passage of *The Spiritual Canticle* he gives some idea of what that silent music was: '... it is tranquil and quiet knowledge, without the sound of voices. And thus there is in it the sweetness of music and the quietude of silence. Accordingly, she says that he Beloved is silent music because in Him she knows and enjoys this symphony of silent music.'

Was his pain also part of that 'silent music'? - a love offering to his Beloved and for the souls he had spent his life guiding and encouraging to the fullness of love. Indeed that pain was so intense that when Fr Antonio was speaking to him John had to ask him to stop because he could not take in what the good father was saying. He could not pray, he could only 'be' - that was his offering of love.

John's experience of love had indeed gone beyond words and anything that the world could express. In the last stanza of *The Living Flame of Love* perhaps the most sublime of his works, he sings:

> How gently and lovingly
> You wake in my heart,
> Where in secret you dwell alone;
> And in your sweet breathing,
> Filled with good and glory,
> How tenderly You swell my heart with love.

Turning to the commentary on this stanza to gain some understanding of this loving indwelling, John cannot give it to us. He has stretched language to its limits already, and he can do no more. 'I do not desire to speak of this inspiration, filled for the soul with good and glory and delicate love of God. I am aware of being incapable of so doing, and were I to try, it might seem less than it is.' God had long dwelt in the secret of his heart, and as the months turned into December he now knew that his time on earth was drawing to a close.

Entering paradise

A week before his death, the doctor, Dr Villarreal, told him that the end was near. John's face lit up. He would soon see the Beloved whom he had sought so assiduously. All through his life he had been aware that God had sought him out far more even than he had sought God, and that soon the 'veil of that sweet encounter' would be torn.

On 13th December John seemed to know that this would be his last day on earth. He asked forgiveness from his brothers for any bad example he had given them. He kept asking what time it was. He received the Sacrament of the Sick, and often kissed his crucifix. He was in intense pain, and the community gathered round him as the Prior began to say the prayers for the dying. John stopped him, and asked him to read from the *Song of Songs*. As it was read John kept repeating, 'what wonderful pearls!' Towards midnight he heard the bell ringing for Matins and asked what it was. When he was told it was for Matins, he replied, 'Glory to God. I shall say them in heaven.' Once more he kissed his crucifix and said, 'Into your hands I commend my spirit.' A few moments after midnight, gently and quietly, he passed out of this world into the arms of his Beloved.

The bride sets all this perfection and preparedness before her Beloved, the Son of God, with the desire that He transfer her from the spiritual marriage, to which He desired to bring her in this Church Militant, to the glorious marriage of the Triumphant. May the most sweet Jesus, Bridegroom of faithful souls, be pleased to bring all who invoke His name to this glorious marriage. To Him be honour and glory, together with the Father and the Holy Spirit, *in saecula saeculorum. Amen.*

Prayers and Writings of John of the Cross

What more do you want, O soul! And what else do you search for outside, when within yourself you possess your riches, delights, satisfaction and kingdom - your Beloved whom you desire and seek? Desire him there, adore him there. Do not go in pursuit of him outside yourself. You will only become distracted and you won't find him, or enjoy him more than by seeking him within you.

———

O blessed Jesus, give me stillness of soul in You. Let Your mighty calmness reign in me. Rule me, O King of Gentleness, King of Peace.

———

O Lord, my God, who will seek You with simple and pure love and not find You are all he desires, for You show Yourself first and go out to meet those who desire You?

———

Lord God, my Beloved, if You remember still my sins in such a way that you do not do what I beg of You, do Your will concerning them, my God, which is what I most desire, and exercise Your goodness and mercy, and You will be known through them. And if it is that You are waiting for my good works so as to hear my prayers through their means, grant them to me, and work them for me, and the sufferings You desire to accept, and let it be done. But if You are not waiting for my works, what is it that makes You wait, my most clement Lord? Why do You delay? For if, after all, I am to receive the grace and mercy which I entreat of You in Your Son, take my mite, since You desire it, and grant me this blessing, since You also desire that.

Who can free himself from lowly manners and limitations if You do not lift him to Yourself, my God, in purity of love? How will a man begotten and nurtured in lowliness rise up to You, Lord, if You do not raise him with Your hand which made him?

You will not take from me, my God, what You once gave me in Your only Son, Jesus Christ, in Whom You gave me all I desire. Hence I rejoice that if I wait for You, You will not delay.

With what procrastinations do you wait, since from this very moment you can love God in your heart?

Mine are the heavens and mine is the earth. Mine are the nations, the just are mine, and mine the sinners. The angels are mine, and the Mother of God, and all things are mine, and God Himself is mine and for me, because Christ is mine and all for me.

What do you ask, the, and seek, my soul? Yours is all

of this, and all is for you. Do not engage yourself in something less, nor pay heed to the crumbs which fall from your Father's table. Go forth and exult in your Glory! Hide yourself in It and rejoice, and you will obtain the supplications of your heart.

———

Oh, then, soul, most beautiful among all creatures, so anxious to know the dwelling place of your Beloved that you may go in quest of Him and be united with Him, now we are telling you that you yourself are His dwelling and His secret chamber and hiding place. This is something of immense gladness for you, to see that all your good and hope is so close to you as to be within you, or better, that you cannot be without Him.

———

If I have already told you all things in My Word, My Son, and if I have no other word, what answer or revelation can I now make that would surpass this? Fasten your eyes on Him alone, because in Him I have spoken and revealed all, and in Him you shall discover even more than you ask for and desire.

———

O Lord my God, who will seek You with simple and pure love and not find You are all he desires, for You show Yourself first and go out to meet those who desire You?

O gentle hand, O delicate touch

O hand, You are as gentle to my soul, which You touch by resting gently, as You would be powerful enough to submerge the entire world if You rested somewhat heavily, for by Your look alone the earth trembles, the nations melt and faint, and the mountains crumble! Oh, then again, great hand, by touching Job somewhat roughly, You were as hard and rigorous with him, as You are friendly and gentle with me; how much more lovingly, graciously, and gently do You permanently touch my soul! You cause death, and You give life, and no one flees from Your hand. For You, O divine life, never kill unless to give life, never wound unless to heal. When You chastise, Your touch is gentle, but it is enough to destroy the world. When You give delight, You rest very firmly, and thus the delight of Your sweetness is immeasurable. You have wounded me in order to cure me, O divine hand, and You have put to death in me what made me lifeless, deprived of God's life in which I now see myself live. You granted this with the liberality of Your generous grace, which You used in contacting me with the touch of the splendour of Your glory and the figure of Your substance, which is Your only begotten Son, through Whom, being Your substance, You touch mightily from one end to the other. And Your only begotten Son, O merciful hand of the Father, is the delicate touch by which You touched me with the force of Your cautery and wounded me.

―――

Endeavour to be inclined always:
not to be easiest, but to the most difficult;
not to the most delightful, but to the harshest;
not to the most gratifying, but to the less pleasant;
not to what means rest for you, but to hard work;
not to the consoling, but to the unconsoling;
not to the most, but to the least;
not to the highest and most precious, but to the lowest and most despised;
not to wanting something, but to wanting nothing;
do not go about looking for the best of temporal things, but for the worst,
and desire to enter into complete nudity, emptiness, and poverty in everything in the world.

―――

To reach satisfaction in all
desire its possession in nothing.
To come to possession all
desire the possession of nothing.
To arrive at being all
desire to be nothing.
To come to the knowledge of all
desire the knowledge of nothing.

To come to the pleasure you have not
you must go by a way in which you enjoy not.
To come to the knowledge you have not
You must go by a way in which you know not.
To come to the possession you have not
you must go by a way in which you possess not.
To come to be what you are not
you must go by a way in which you are not.
When you turn toward something
you cease to cast yourself upon the all.
For to go from all to the all
you must deny yourself of all in all.
And when you come to the possession of the all
you must possess it without wanting anything.
Because if you desire to have something in all
your treasure in God is not purely your all.
In this nakedness the spirit finds
its quietude and rest.
For in coveting nothing,
nothing raises it up
and nothing weighs it down,
because it is in the centre of its humility.
When it covets something
in this very desire it is wearied.

Maxims of John of the Cross

O sweetest love of God, so little known, he who has found its veins is at rest!

A soul enkindled with love is a gentle, meek, humble, and patient soul.

Lord my God, You are not a stranger to him who does not estrange himself from You. How do they say that it is You who absent Yourself?

At the evening of life, you will be examined in love. Learn to love as God desires to be loved and abandon your own ways of acting.

Consider that God reigns only in the peaceful and disinterested soul.

Keep spiritually tranquil in a loving attentiveness to God, and when it is necessary to speak, let it be with the same calm and peace.

Enter within yourself and work in the presence of your Spouse, Who is ever present loving you.

The Father spoke one Word, which was His Son, and this Word He always speaks in eternal silence, and in silence must It be heard by the soul.

Seek in reading and you will find in meditation, knock in prayer and it will be opened to you in contemplation.

Prayers to John of the Cross

Saint John of the Cross, in the darkness of your worst moments, when you were alone and persecuted, you found God. Help me to have faith that God is there especially in the times when God seems absent and far away. Amen

Lord, you endowed St John of the Cross with a spirit of self-denial and love of the cross. By following his example may we come to the eternal vision of your glory. We ask this through Christ our Lord. Amen.

Endnote

[1] One of the best introductions to John's life and writings, related to today, is *The Impact of God* by Iain Matthew. He gives many beautifully translated little quotes from John's writings, and a good way into his Works is to look up the quotes that Iain gives and read them in context. Following the poetry's stanzas, the commentaries are also in sections, so it easy to read them in short bursts.

CTS

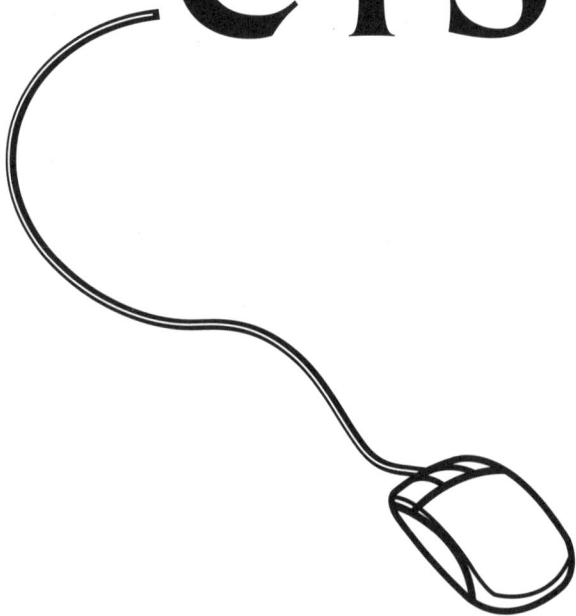

... now online
www.cts-online.org.uk